VOCAL SHEET MUSIC

WOMEN'S EDITION

SINGER + PIANO/GUITAR

BROADWAY FAVORITES

D0503905

ISBN 978-1-5400-1534-1

HAL•LEONARD®

Visit Hal Leonard Online at
www.halleonard.com

Contact Us:
Hal Leonard
7777 West Bluemound Road
Milwaukee, WI 53213
Email: info@halleonard.com

In Europe contact:
Hal Leonard Europe Limited
42 Wigmore Street
Marylebone, London, W1U 2RN
Email: info@halleonardeurope.com

In Australia contact:
Hal Leonard Australia Pty. Ltd.
4 Lentara Court
Cheltenham, Victoria, 3192 Australia
Email: info@halleonard.com.au

ASTONISHING
from the Broadway Musical LITTLE WOMEN

Music by JASON HOWLAND
Lyrics by MINDI DICKSTEIN

BURN
from HAMILTON

Words and Music by
LIN-MANUEL MIRANDA

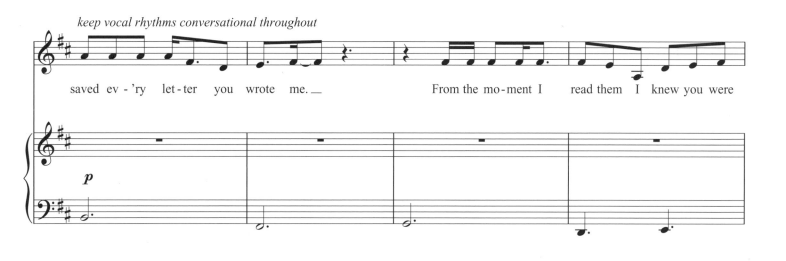

saved ev-'ry let-ter you wrote me. From the mo-ment I read them I knew you were

mine. You said you were mine. I thought you were ___ mine. ___

BEYOND MY WILDEST DREAMS

from THE LITTLE MERMAID – A BROADWAY MUSICAL

Music by ALAN MENKEN
Lyrics by GLENN SLATER

With excitement

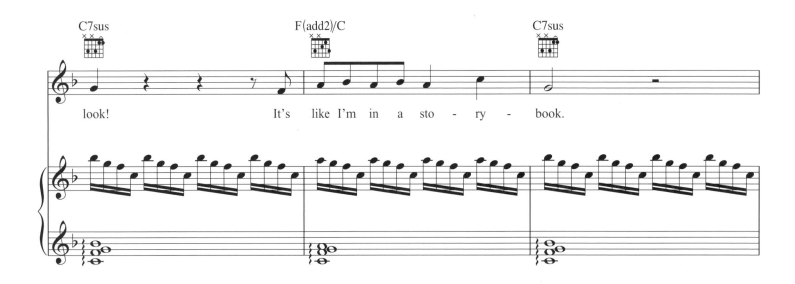

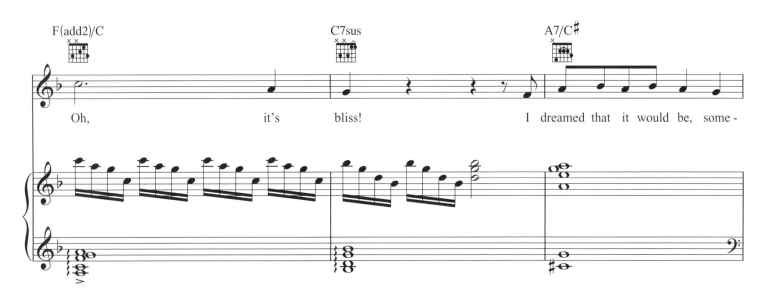

wished and won-dered what I'd do here. Wished and prayed and

pic - tured what I'd see. Prayed, and wow! My

pray'rs are com - ing true here. Look at it all, look how it gleams!

Love - ly be-yond my wild - est dreams.

A CHANGE IN ME

from BEAUTY AND THE BEAST: THE BROADWAY MUSICAL

Music by ALAN MENKEN
Words by TIM RICE

DEFYING GRAVITY
from the Broadway Musical WICKED

Music and Lyrics by
STEPHEN SCHWARTZ

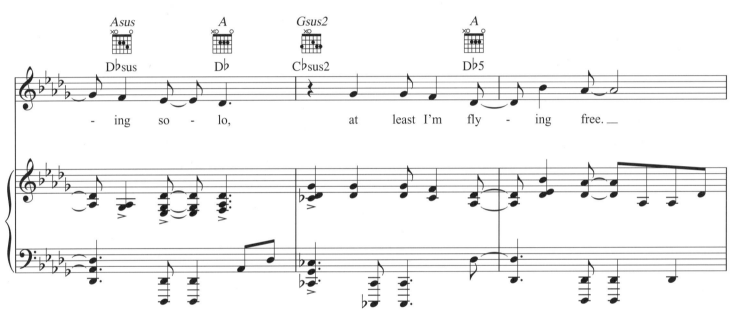

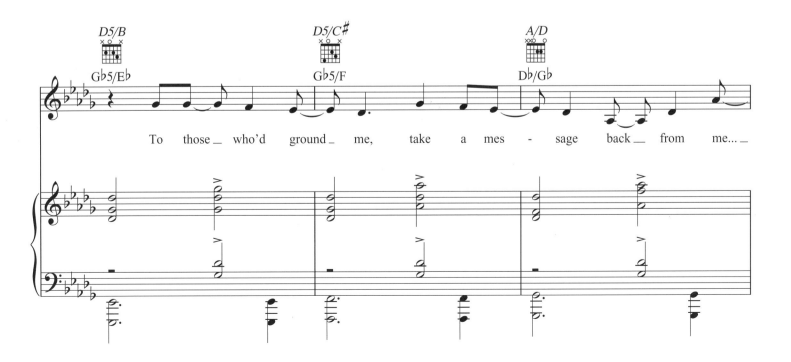

FLY, FLY AWAY

from CATCH ME IF YOU CAN

Lyrics by SCOTT WITTMAN and MARC SHAIMAN
Music by MARC SHAIMAN

bye, good-bye. _____ No need to tell me why, my ba-by. _____

May-be it's be-cause you'll fly back home to me one day. _____

Ba-by, when you're in the clouds, please keep a look-out. _____

May-be, dar-lin', find a hide-a-way for _ you and I, _____ you and I.

FOR THE FIRST TIME IN FOREVER

from FROZEN: THE BROADWAY MUSICAL

Music and Lyrics by KRISTEN ANDERSON-LOPEZ
and ROBERT LOPEZ

With excitement ($\quarternote$ = 98)

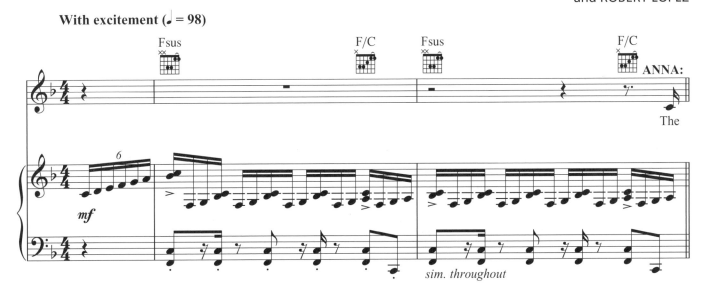

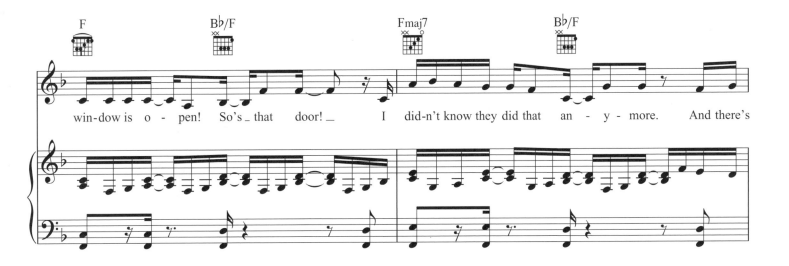

D♭

on a show,   make   one wrong move and ev -'ry - one will

A♭5   **A♭m/C♭**

(8va)---

E♭5   **D♭/F**

know.   But it's on - ly for to -

G♭   **G♭/F♭**   **A♭/E♭**   **A♭/G♭**

ANNA:
It's on - ly for to - day! _____   It's ag - o - ny to wait!

day.

ELSA:
It's ag - o - ny to wait.

WOMEN:
Ooh _____   Ooh _____

MEN:
Ooh _____   Ooh _____

mp *cresc.*

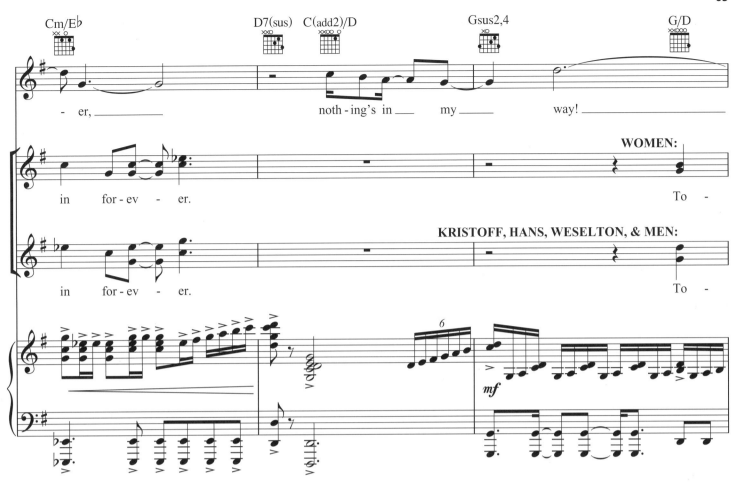

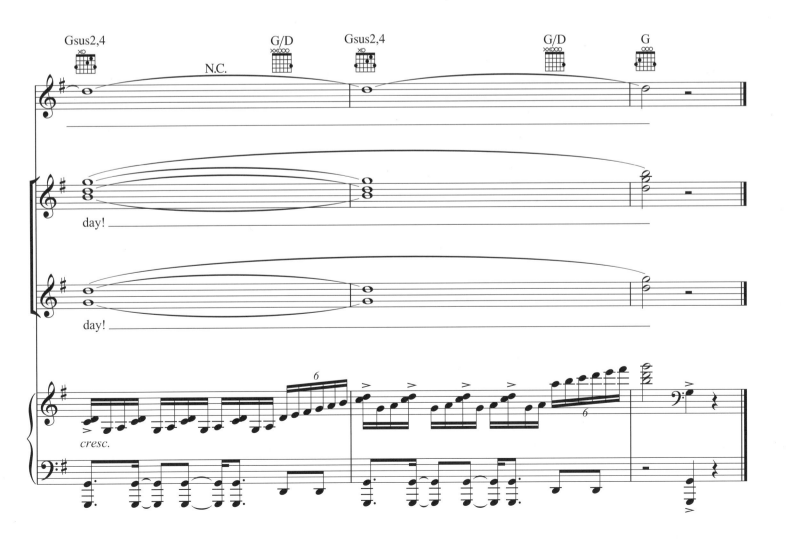

GIMME GIMME
from THOROUGHLY MODERN MILLIE

Music by JEANINE TESORI
Lyrics by DICK SCANLAN

THE HISTORY OF WRONG GUYS

from KINKY BOOTS

Words and Music by
CYNTHIA LAUPER

I MISS THE MOUNTAINS
from NEXT TO NORMAL

Lyrics by BRIAN YORKEY
Music by TOM KITT

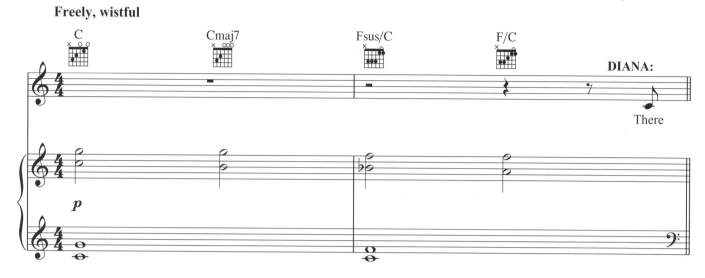

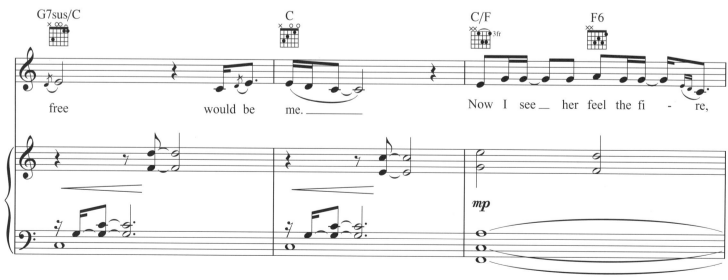

IF YOU KNEW MY STORY
from BRIGHT STAR

Music by STEPHEN MARTIN
and EDIE BRICKELL
Lyrics by EDIE BRICKELL

Easy 2

tell _____ me. _____ I'm _____

not _____ a - lone. _____

Tell _____ me _____ I'm _____

not _____ a - lone. _____ Man - y

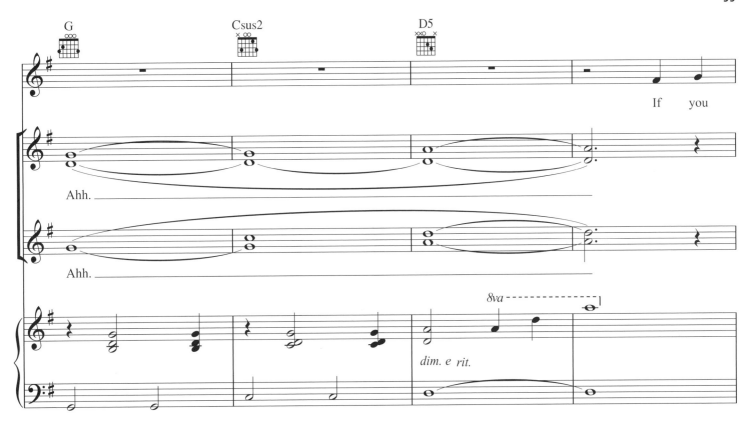

Slower

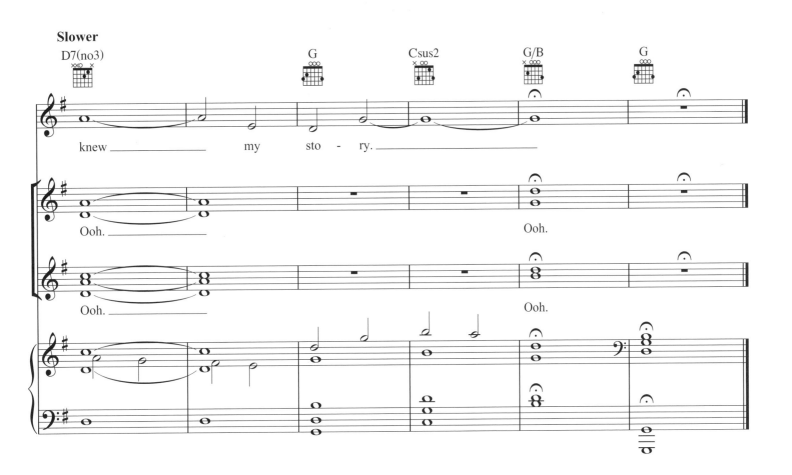

JENNY'S BLUES
from IT SHOULDA BEEN YOU

Words by BRIAN HARGROVE
Music by BARBARA ANSELMI

Colla voce, Swing 8ths

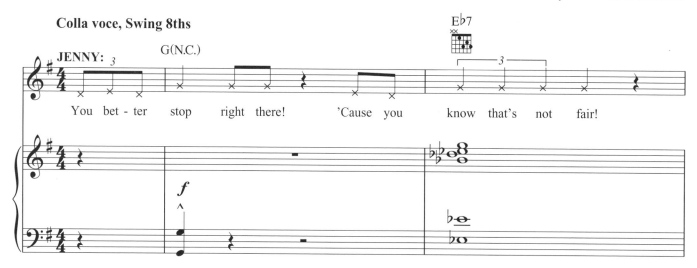

You bet-ter stop right there! 'Cause you know that's not fair!

I ____ pulled this off with-out a glitch! So say good-bye, I'm done. I'm gon-na

have some fun. I'm tired of be-ing your bitch!

Slightly slower and building

I've spent my whole damn life _____ just wait - in'. _____

_____ Oth - ers danced while I just sat _____ on the shelf. _

I have lived to

please, ain't no _____ de - bat - in'. _

MAMA WHO BORE ME

from SPRING AWAKENING

Music by DUNCAN SHEIK
Lyrics by STEVEN SATER

LET IT GO
from FROZEN: THE BROADWAY MUSICAL

Music and Lyrics by KRISTEN ANDERSON-LOPEZ
and ROBERT LOPEZ

Be the good girl you al-ways have to be. Con-ceal. Don't feel.

Don't let them know. Well, now

they know. Let it go, let it go.

Can't hold it back an-y-more. Let it go,

PINK
from WAR PAINT

Music by SCOTT FRANKEL
Lyrics by MICHAEL KORIE

More regular

po - sy pink, on Ma - mie Ei - sen - how - er's lips.

Pink on Mrs. __ As - tor's roots and tips. Pink, the box - es

pack - aged with a bow that cost more than the lo - tion.

Pink. That flush of ar - dor in a man's em - brace. My would-be

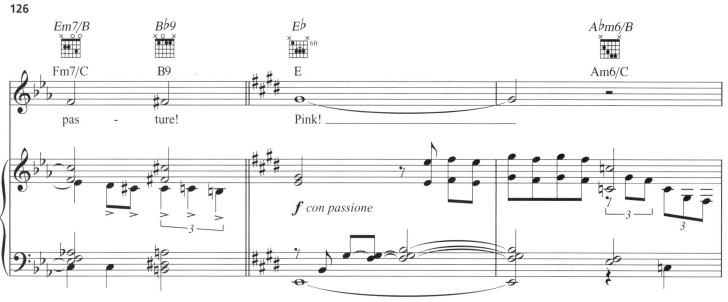

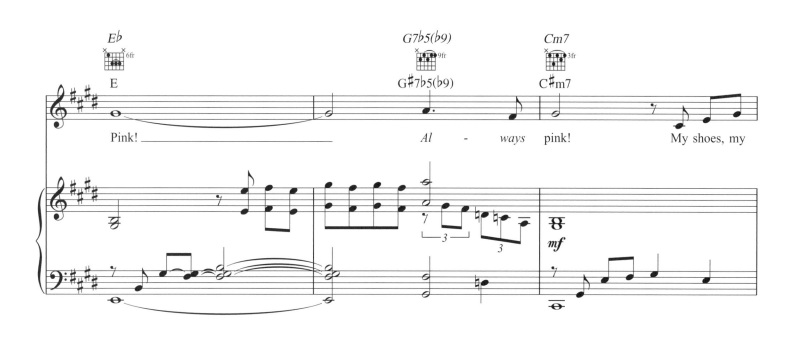

POPULAR
from the Broadway Musical WICKED

Music and Lyrics by
STEPHEN SCHWARTZ

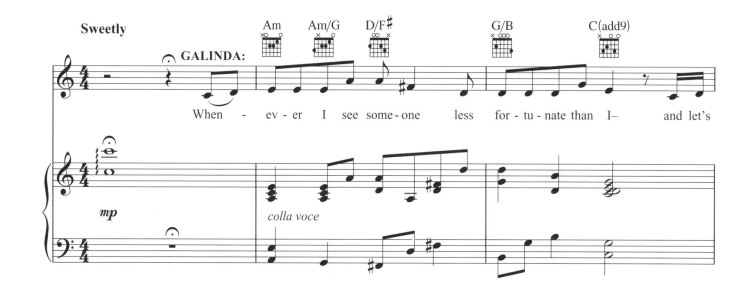

Sweetly

GALINDA:

When-ev-er I see some-one less for-tu-nate than I— and let's

face it, who is-n't less for-tu-nate than I? —My ten-der heart tends to start to

bleed And when some-one needs a make-o-ver, I sim-ply have to take o-ver; I

THERE'S A FINE, FINE LINE

from the Broadway Musical AVENUE Q

Music and Lyrics by ROBERT LOPEZ
and JEFF MARX

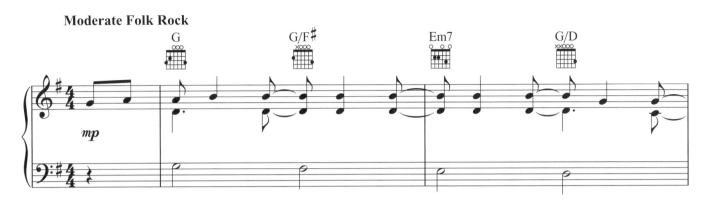

Moderate Folk Rock

KATE MONSTER:

There's a fine, fine line

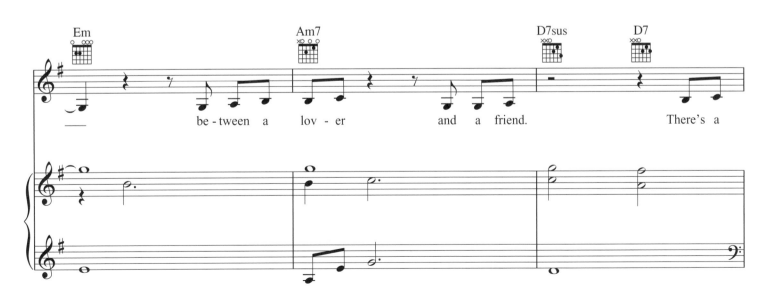

be-tween a lov-er and a friend. There's a

PULLED

from THE ADDAMS FAMILY

Words and Music by
ANDREW LIPPA

Misterioso

Dm | E/D

Dm | E/D | Dm

WEDNESDAY:
I don't have a sun-ny dis-po-si-tion. I'm not known for be-ing too a-

E/D | Gm | Dm/F

mused. My de-mean-or's locked in one po-si-tion. See my

Em7♭5 | A7sus | A7 | Dm

face? I'm en-thused.

Sud-den-ly, how-ev-er, I've been

8va

mf

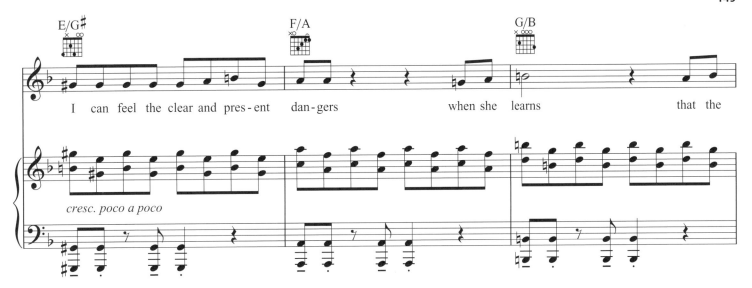

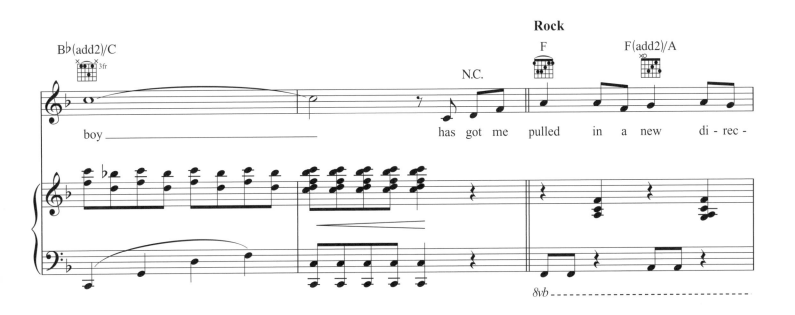

RIGHT HAND MAN

from SOMETHING ROTTEN!

Words and Music by WAYNE KIRKPATRICK
and KAREY KIRKPATRICK

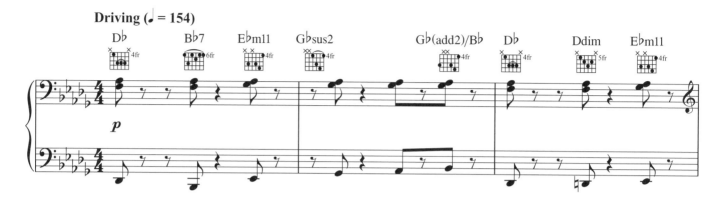

If you ev-er got in trou-ble I would be there on the dou-ble, just to

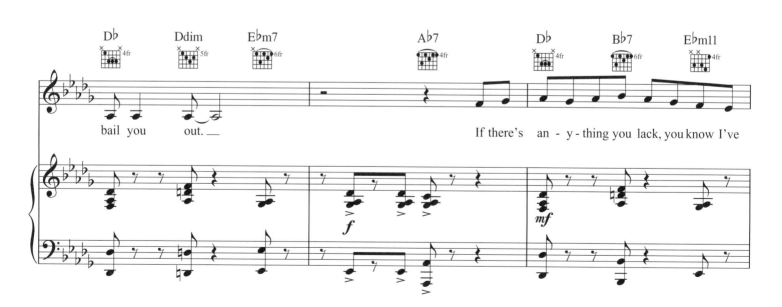

bail you out. ___ If there's an-y-thing you lack, you know I've

SHE USED TO BE MINE
from WAITRESS THE MUSICAL

Words and Music by
SARA BAREILLES

SHOW OFF
from THE DROWSY CHAPERONE

Words and Music by LISA LAMBERT
and GREG MORRISON

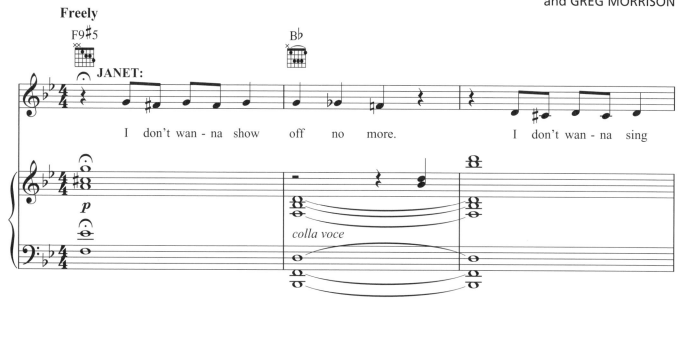

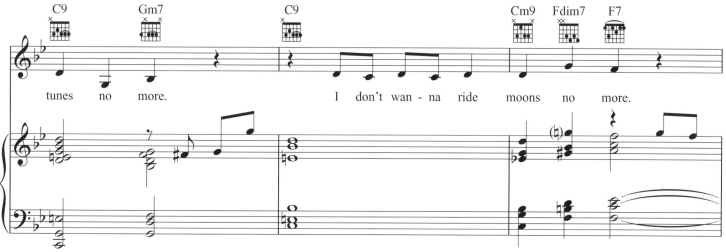

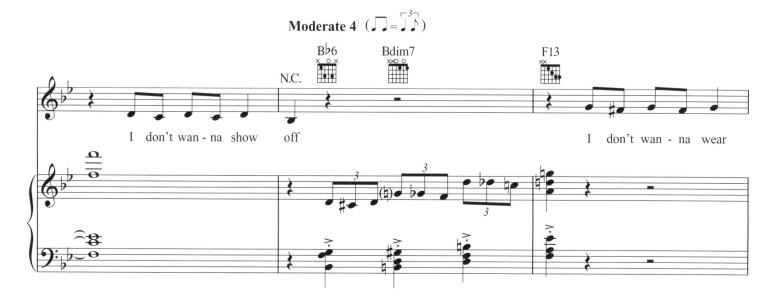

STILL HURTING
from THE LAST FIVE YEARS

Music and Lyrics by
JASON ROBERT BROWN

THAT WOULD BE ENOUGH
from HAMILTON

Words and Music by
LIN-MANUEL MIRANDA

WATCH WHAT HAPPENS

from NEWSIES THE MUSICAL

Music by ALAN MENKEN
Lyrics by JACK FELDMAN

WITH YOU

from GHOST THE MUSICAL

Words and Music by GLEN BALLARD,
DAVID ALLAN STEWART and BRUCE JOEL RUBIN

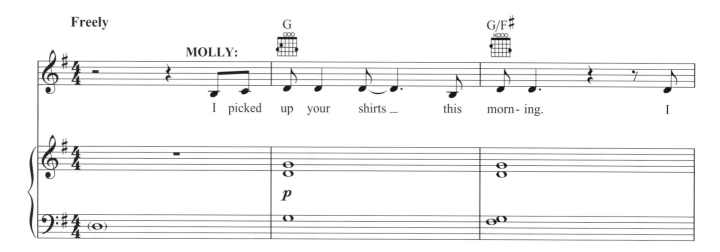

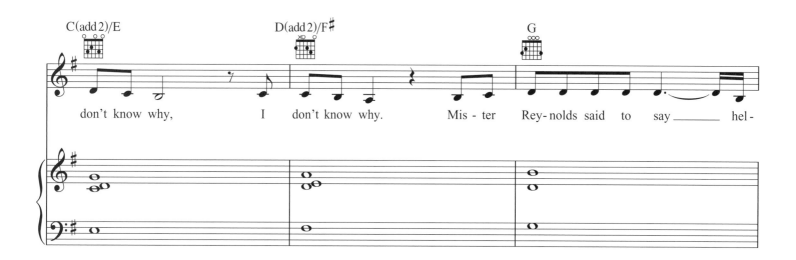

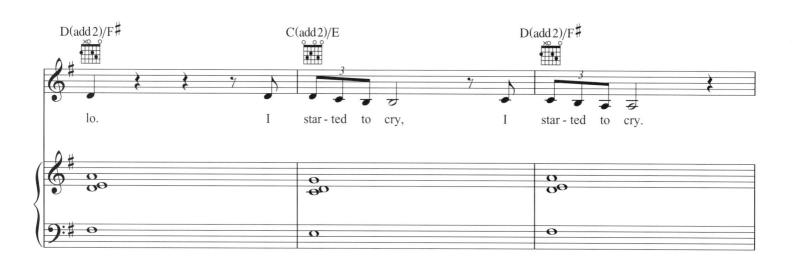

THE SINGER'S MUSICAL THEATRE ANTHOLOGY

The World's Most Trusted Source for Great Theatre Literature for Singing Actors

Compiled and Edited by Richard Walters

The songs in this series are vocal essentials from classic and contemporary shows – ideal for the auditioning, practicing or performing vocalist. Each of the eighteen books contains songs chosen because of their appropriateness to that particular voice type. All selections are in their authentic form, excerpted from the original vocal scores. Each volume features notes about the shows and songs. There is no duplication between volumes.

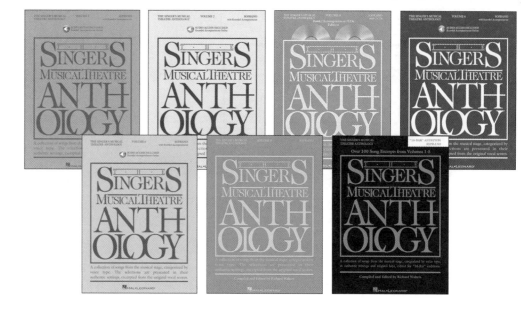

VOLUME 1

SOPRANO
(REVISED EDITION)
00000483 Book/Online Audio $42.99
00361071 Book Only.....................$22.99
00740227 2 Accompaniment CDs..$22.99

MEZZO-SOPRANO/BELTER
(REVISED EDITION)
00000484 Book/Online Audio $42.99
00361072 Book Only.....................$22.99
00740230 2 Accompaniment CDs..$22.99

TENOR
(REVISED EDITION)
00000485 Book/Online Audio $42.99
00361073 Book Only.....................$22.99
00740233 2 Accompaniment CDs..$24.99

BARITONE/BASS
(REVISED EDITION)
00000486 Book/Online Audio $42.99
00361074 Book Only.....................$24.99
00740236 2 Accompaniment CDs..$22.99

DUETS
00000487 Book/Online Audio $42.99
00361075 Book Only.....................$22.99
00740239 2 Accompaniment CDs..$22.99

VOLUME 2

SOPRANO
(REVISED EDITION)
00000488 Book/Online Audio $44.99
00747066 Book Only.....................$22.99
00740228 2 Accompaniment CDs..$24.99

MEZZO-SOPRANO/BELTER
(REVISED EDITION)
00000489 Book/Online Audio $42.99
00747031 Book Only.....................$22.99
00740231 2 Accompaniment CDs..$22.99

TENOR
00000490 Book/Online Audio $44.99
00747032 Book Only.....................$24.99
00740234 2 Accompaniment CDs..$24.99

BARITONE/BASS
00000491 Book/Online Audio $44.99
00747033 Book Only.....................$22.99
00740237 2 Accompaniment CDs..$22.99

DUETS
00000492 Book/Online Audio $42.99
00740331 Book Only.....................$24.99
00740240 2 Accompaniment CDs..$24.99

VOLUME 3

SOPRANO
00000493 Book/Online Audio $42.99
00740122 Book Only.....................$22.99
00740229 2 Accompaniment CDs..$24.99

MEZZO SOPRANO/BELTER
00000494 Book/Online Audio $44.99
00740123 Book Only.....................$22.99
00740232 2 Accompaniment CDs..$24.99

TENOR
00000495 Book/Online Audio $42.99
00740124 Book Only.....................$22.99
00740235 2 Accompaniment CDs..$22.99

BARITONE/BASS
00000496 Book/Online Audio $42.99
00740125 Book Only.....................$24.99
00740238 2 Accompaniment CDs..$24.99

VOLUME 4

SOPRANO
00000497 Book/Online Audio $42.99
00000393 Book Only.....................$22.99
00000397 2 Accompaniment CDs..$24.99

MEZZO SOPRANO/BELTER
00000498 Book/Online Audio $42.99
00000394 Book Only.....................$22.99
00000398 2 Accompaniment CDs..$22.99

TENOR
00000499 Book/Online Audio $42.99
00000395 Book Only.....................$22.99
00000399 2 Accompaniment CDs..$24.99

BARITONE/BASS
00000799 Book/Online Audio $42.99
00000396 Book Only.....................$24.99
00000401 2 Accompaniment CDs..$24.99

VOLUME 5

SOPRANO
00001162 Book/Online Audio $42.99
00001151 Book Only.....................$24.99
00001157 2 Accompaniment CDs..$22.99

MEZZO-SOPRANO/BELTER
00001163 Book/Online Audio $42.99
00001152 Book Only.....................$24.99
00001158 2 Accompaniment CDs..$24.99

TENOR
00001164 Book/Online Audio $42.99
00001153 Book Only.....................$24.99
00001159 2 Accompaniment CDs..$22.99

BARITONE/BASS
00001165 Book/Online Audio $42.99
00001154 Book Only.....................$24.99
00001160 2 Accompaniment CDs..$24.99

VOLUME 6

SOPRANO
00145264 Book/Online Audio $42.99
00145258 Book Only.....................$22.99
00151246 2 Accompaniment CDs..$22.99

MEZZO-SOPRANO/BELTER
00145265 Book/Online Audio $42.99
00145259 Book Only.....................$22.99
00151247 2 Accompaniment CDs..$22.99

TENOR
00145266 Book/Online Audio $42.99
00145260 Book Only.....................$22.99
00151248 2 Accompaniment CDs..$22.99

BARITONE/BASS
00145267 Book/Online Audio $42.99
00145261 Book Only.....................$24.99
00151249 2 Accompaniment CDs..$22.99

THE SINGER'S MUSICAL THEATRE ANTHOLOGY – "16-BAR" AUDITION

00230039 Soprano Edition $24.99
00230040 Mezzo-Soprano Edition .$24.99

TEEN'S EDITION

SOPRANO
00230047 Book/Online Audio $39.99
00230043 Book Only.....................$22.99
00230051 2 Accompaniment CDs..$22.99

MEZZO-SOPRANO/ALTO/BELTER
00230048 Book/Online Audio $42.99
00230044 Book Only.....................$21.99
00230052 2 Accompaniment CDs..$22.99

TENOR
00230049 Book/Online Audio $39.99
00230045 Book Only.....................$21.99
00230053 2 Accompaniment CDs..$24.99

BARITONE/BASS
00230050 Book/Online Audio $39.99
00230046 Book Only.....................$19.99
00230054 2 Accompaniment CDs..$24.99

HAL•LEONARD®

Prices, contents, and availability are subject to change without notice.

Please visit **www.halleonard.com**
for complete contents listings.